Memories of STOCKPORT

Foreword

Memories of Stockport is a compilation of photographs spanning the period from around 1930 to the very early 1970s. This period of time is chosen intentionally, and the majority of images contained in this book are from the post war years.

The reason for this is deliberate: *Memories of Stockport* is not intended to be a history book, with abstract scenes from bygone days, it is meant to be a catalyst for rekindling memories, for people who were there themselves as well as for those who just want to know what life was like for their elders.

So if you remember Merseyway when it was a road, not a shopping precinct; or perhaps you were in town the day that the Queen Mother visited in 1960, or maybe knew someone who worked at Avro, Woodford when the firm was making everything from Ansons to Vulcans, or then again you might remember when Stockport County were go-go-going up to the Third Division in 1967....well then there will be something in these pages that will bring memories flooding back.

Whatever you age, I hope that you enjoy reading *Memories of Stockport* as much as I have enjoyed compiling it!

Mark Smith
Publisher

The Queen Mother's visit to Stockport in June 1960 brought hundreds of people out onto the streets around the town centre.

Published in November 1996 by:
True North Books
Dean Clough
Halifax HX3 5AX Tel: 01422 344344
Repro. by Transgraphic Ltd., Morley.
Printed by Joseph Ward ColourPrint Ltd., Dewsbury

Memories of Stockport
ISBN 1 900 463 55 5

Copyright: True North Holdings
Copyright of Library pictures: Stockport Libraries

All rights reserved. No part of this publication may be reproduced, stored in a retrieval system or transmitted in any form without the permission of the publishers

£4.99 nett

Memories of STOCKPORT

Contents

Section one	Events
Section two	Avro, Woodford
Section three	At work
Section four	Changing town centre
Section five	At war
Section six	The Stockport Air Disaster
Section seven	Football memories
Section eight	Shopping

Crowds of shoppers mill around in Stockport Market, circa 1965.

Acknowledgments

The publishers would like to thank the following people for their contribution in making this book possible: David Isaac and Ros Lathbury of Stockport Libraries, Peter Greenwood, group editor of the Stockport Express Advertiser series and Liz Pearce, librarian for the newspaper group. Around 20 pictures from the Stockport Express/Advertiser group appear in this book, mainly in the events section. Thanks to Richard Harnwell who provided the Stockport County pictures as well as the captions that accompany them. Harry Holmes kindly made the "Avro" pictures available to the publishers as well as providing the background information that appears in the Avro section, for which the publishers are very grateful. Thanks are also due to the many local companies who allowed us to "tell their story" in the book - indeed, the majority of these businesses are local, long established concerns and as such are part of the history of the area. By supporting this book they also allow us to keep the price to a relatively modest level. Finally, thanks to Andrew Hales for organising the advertising content.

Events

Stockport has enjoyed several royal visits over the past few decades, but undoubtedly one of the most popular was the visit of the Queen Mother in the summer of 1960. The main reason for her presence in the town was for Her Royal Highness was to visit Christy and Co. Ltd, the local hat makers with the national reputation. This picture captures the Queen Mother's arrival at Edgeley Station, 10.45 on 22nd June 1960. She is shown being greeted by the mayor and mayoress with the town clerk in the background.

Memories of STOCKPORT

The pictures on this double page spread capture the excitement and anticipation of local "royal watchers" who turned out in their thousands for the Queens Mother's visit on the 22nd of June, 1960.

The two views are actually taken within a few minutes of each other from both ends of Great Underbank. The Queen Mother's route took her from Edgeley Station, via the town centre, and then to Christy and Co.'s premises. The presence of summer dresses in these two pictures provides ample evidence of the weather on the day, which was sunny with a light breeze. The amount of bunting that local shopkeepers had erected is also impressive.

Stockport Express

Memories of STOCKPORT

Royal visits have always generated large crowds in Stockport, and as well as this particular visit, locals turned out in droves to see the Queen, when she visited in 1968 and Prince Charles, when he attended Marple Memorial Park in 1981. But, the level of interest and size of crowds have tended to diminish in the post-war period. One of the theories put forward to explain this is the fact that television enables everyone to witness a visit, without actually attending. Indeed, the coronation of Queen Elizabeth in 1953 was the first national constitutional event to be seen by millions of television viewers. But in 1960, the crowds were on the street, not in front of the telly!

Stockport Express

Memories of STOCKPORT

Left: The culmination of the Queen Mother's June 1960 visit to Stockport was when she attended a reception at the Town Hall. The crowds were certainly out in force next to the Town Hall steps, and can be seen engaging in some good-natured banter with the two Police Constables on duty there. The Policewoman would have been a relatively rare sight in the early 1960s. Wellington Road South can be seen stretching away towards Mersey Square. *Below left:* More crowds waiting to catch a glimpse of the Queen Mother in 1960. *Below:* A different Royal visit is shown in this May 1968 picture, when the Queen came to Stockport to witness the achievements of the initiative to clean up the town - dubbed Operation Spring Clean.

The Queen was taken on a guided tour of areas that had been cleaned up and renovated and unlike the June 1960 Royal visit, the Queen's day in Stockport saw the weather dominated by drissle.

Memories of STOCKPORT

Below: The infants class of Woodley Council School pose for their 1925 class photograph. Until 1903 education in Stockport was provided by Voluntary School managers. After this time there was a movement towards the local authority taking over these schools, which then became Council Schools, such as the primary school at Woodley. By 1947 there were 16 Council Schools in the district.

Above: A group of Stockport children about to set off on a seaside trip in the mid 1930s.

Memories of STOCKPORT

Robinson Street, Edgeley, 1953. Bunting, flags and the look of celebration on the faces of the people in this happy scene give a clue to the event - the coronation of Queen Elizabeth the Second. The weather was wet and windy (as can be seen by the bunting fluttering in Robinson Street). At Woodbank Park events had been planned from dawn 'til dusk, but instead of hundreds turning out, dozens actually made it on the day. But in the Town Hall over 1800 people paid for a ticket to see the television relay of the entire ceremony. The mayor was at Westminster Abbey and enjoyed an excellent view, but the mayoress stayed in Stockport and toured the local street parties. For the majority of people though, the day was spent indoors, watching the event take place on tiny black and white television screens. Few homes had them, but those families that did found themselves playing host to grateful neighbours. In retrospect, it can be seen that this was the day that the television age really began.

Avro, Woodford

In 1908 Alliot Verdon Roe became the first Englishman to fly, when he few his flimsy biplane for 150 yards. Two years later the company he set up to manufacture aeroplanes was given his name, AV Roe - Avro was born. Expansion of his business saw the need for premises with an airfield alongside, and thus Avro opened the airfield at Woodford in 1925, with a flying display as part of the opening ceremony. The company shared the aerodrome with the Lancashire Aero Club and these two organisations thrilled over 5,000 members of the public with a breathtaking air show. The picture on the bottom right was taken on the opening day of Avro Woodford. Landing is an Avro Gosport while a DeHavilland Moth is in the foreground and in the distance can be seen a wooden fort which was often successfully '"bombed" by the R.A.F. at future air displays.

The establishment of Woodford as an aerodrome was not without its difficulties for Avro as the facility had no water or electricity available and, in fact, the latter was not supplied until 1933! The hangar, shown above in 1928, survives to this day as part of the Flight Sheds Complex. Woodford's massive *New Assembly* facility covers over one million square feet and is an ideal aircraft production facility. The airfield, with its 7,000 feet main runway, is in the distance. The photograph was taken in June 1958.

Memories of STOCKPORT

The first Shackletons on the production line at Woodford in March 1950. In the background are four Lancasters in for refurbishment and, at the far end, an Avro Tudor airliner. Following the end of the war several Lancasters were utilised by Coastal Command but it soon became clear that these heroes of the war were now inadequate for the task, and a larger maritime patrol aeroplane was needed. This resulted in the introduction of the Shackleton, with the first deliveries to Coastal Command in the early part of 1951. The Shackleton enjoyed a long lifespan and continued in service until the early 1970s, when it was replaced by the Nimrod as the front line reconnaissance aircraft used by the RAF.

Memories of STOCKPORT

Right: Two versions of the Avro Athena advanced training aircraft are seen outside the Woodford Flight Sheds in October 1949. On the left is the Club House with the old wartime hangars, which had been erected in 1925, in the background. The other aircraft in the photograph is an Avro Anson. This particular aircraft would have been a regular sight in the skies over Stockport for many years. The first Anson went into service in 1935 with the last example delivered to the RAF in May 1952. In total over 11,000 Ansons were built.

Right: Lancaster Bombers awaiting test flying or delivery at Woodford in October 1942. The factory was turning out these aircraft at an average rate of seven per day. Avro's factories at Chadderton and Woodford can be credited with many major achievements in the production of aircraft both during and after the Second World War. Between the two factories over 7,500 Lancaster bombers were produced. Indeed, Avro Lancasters delivered over two thirds of the total tonnage of bombs dropped by the RAF from 1942 to the end of the war.

Memories of
STOCKPORT

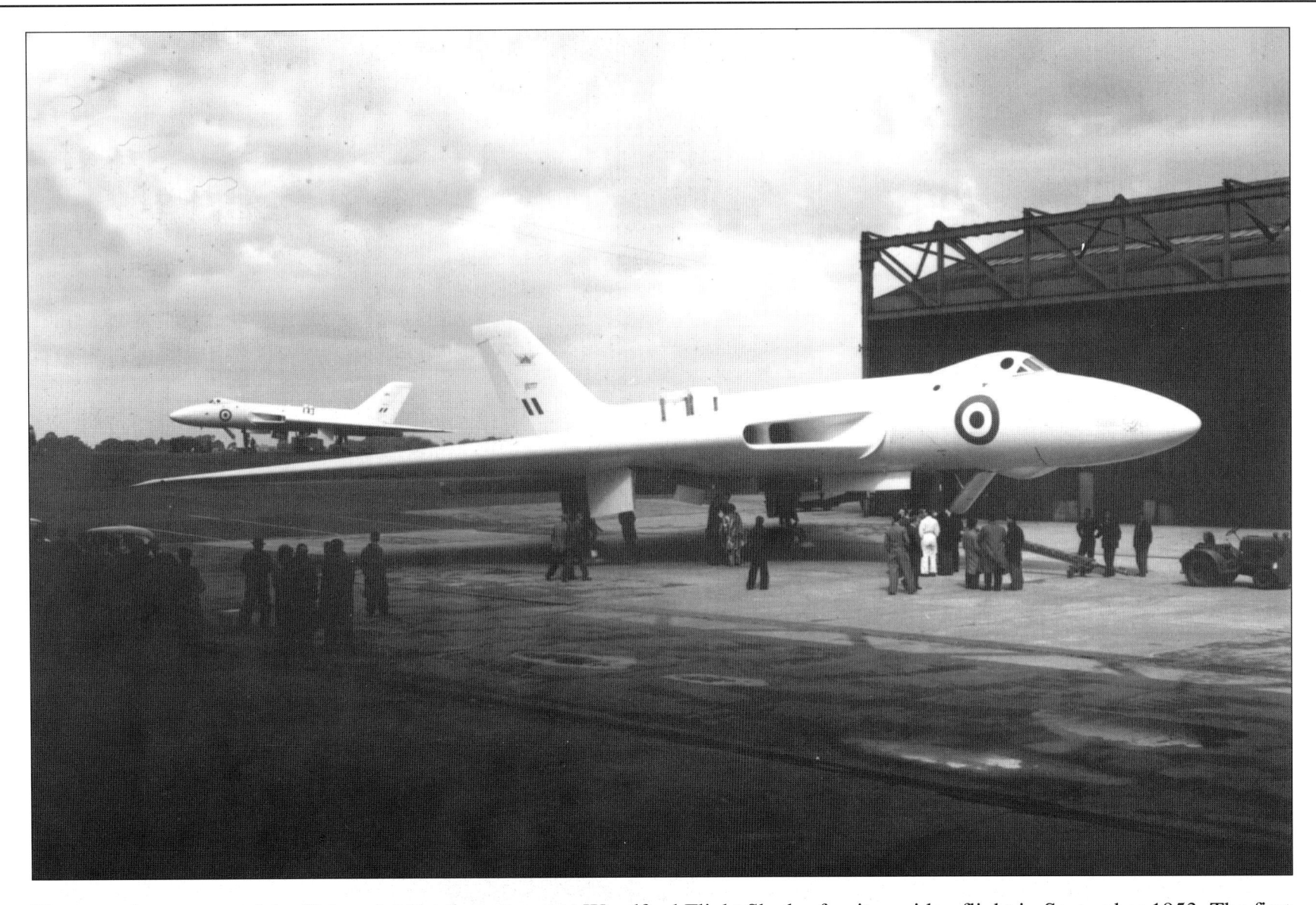

The second prototype of the Vulcan Jet Bomber returns to Woodford Flight Sheds after its maiden flight in September 1953. The first prototype can be seen in the background and had made its first flight on August 30th, 1952. The Vulcan became the backbone of the RAF Strike Command and was central to the country's air defences for over two decades. The "delta-wing" shape of the Vulcan, coupled with its considerable size, is still striking today. In 1952 it must have been an amazing sight for local people, many of who would have witnessed it on test flights.

Memories of STOCKPORT

The world's most reliable turboprop engine, the Rolls-Royce Dart, powered the Avro 748 and the orders kept the Woodford production lines busy throughout the 1960s and 70s. Eventually almost 400 of this reliable airliner were sold in fifty countries throughout the world. The Woodford airfield is capable of accommodating all the aircraft operated by the RAF, as well as most large civil aircraft. This is due to the size of its main runway, which is some 7500 feet long.

Memories of STOCKPORT

Frederic Robinson Limited - a tradition of brewing in Stockport.

The Robinson's story begins in September 1838 when William Robinson bought the Unicorn Inn, Lower Hillgate, Stockport (demolished in 1935), from Samuel Hole and began running it as a retail business. His younger son Frederic joined him in 1865 and started to brew his own beer, but he soon branched out into the wholesale business - his first customer was Mrs. Lamb of the Bridge Inn, Chestergate.

On the 3rd May 1876, shortly after his father's death he purchased the Railway at Marple Bridge (rebuilt in the 1930s and since renamed the Royal Scot) - and so began the growth of the estate.

In 1878 Frederic's eldest son, William, joined him aged 14, by which time they owned two licenced houses and a horse and dray - the beginnings of the distribution fleet. When Frederic died in 1890 he was the owner of 12 licenced houses. The business then passed to his widow Emma. April 1915 saw the acquisition of John Heginbotham's of Stalybridge.

By 1920, when the business became a limited company, William had been joined by his sons Frederic, Edgar (later Sir John) and Cecil. Further acquisitions followed and in 1933 William died, to be succeeded as Chairman by Edgar.

In the years that followed, interrupted by the second World War, many rural houses were bought, resulting in the number of delightful houses still owned by the company. The early 1950s saw Edgar's three sons Peter, Dennis and David join the company and by the late 1960s Frederic had retired. This time coincided with a revived interest in real ale which saw the company consolidate brewing at the Unicorn Brewery in Stockport. A bottling plant at Bredbury was also built, opening in 1975. In 1978 Sir John died suddenly at the Brewery. The board was then reconstituted with Cecil (who died in 1980) as the company's first president, Peter as Chairman, Dennis and David. In 1982 the old established brewer, Hartleys (Ulverston) Limited was acquired, and more recently further development has been completed at Bredbury.

Traditional draught beers are still Robinson's mainstay, although these are now joined by take-home packs of bottles and cans. Whilst the area covered by the brewery extends from North Wales to the Lakes, the town of Stockport is still very much home to Robinson's, as it has been for over a century and a half.

Steamers to the left and the motorised Leyland fleet at the Loading stage, Unicorn Brewery circa 1920.

At Work

Right: The Stockport Viaduct has been a part of the town's landscape since it was built in 1840. This view of Gas Street was taken in the mid 1960s and would have served to reinforce the perception held by some that Stockport was an industrial town with its fair share of gritty landscape. The viaduct was treated to a £3 million clean up in the late 1980s which restored the original colour of its bricks after nearly a century-and-a-half of grime had accumulated.

Below: This 1960s view over Portwood is dominated by the "Green Giant" gasometer, with the Stockport Power Station running a close second. The gasometer was built in 1930 and was held to be the ultimate in gas storage systems for its time. Unlike the normal gasometer design which utilised rising and falling walls, the Portwood gasometer had a huge internal piston which rose as the pressure of gas beneath it increased. It was 255 feet high and christened the Green Giant because of the colour scheme that adorned its walls for many year, although it was repainted grey in 1983. This most noticeable landmark was demolished in 1988.

Memories of STOCKPORT

F. Bamford & Co. Ltd. - Stockport engineering propelling ships worldwide.

The story of the local marine engineering company, F Bamford & Co. Ltd began in Waterloo Road, Stockport, in 1903, when founder Fred Bamford joined forces with a man named Kershaw to manufacture marine engines.

The business prospered but Bamford found that his customers wanted a complete drive train package so he undertook the manufacture of propellers. Soon many other companies involved in the marine engineering industry passed their propeller manufacturing work onto Bamfords, and by the start of the First World War the firm's sales of propellers had overtaken those of engines. Fred Bamford became an acknowledged expert in the hydrodynamics of propellers and after the end of the Great War the firm thrived as a result of concentrating in this area of marine engineering.

The company achieved some notable successes in this field, including the manufacture of the propellers fitted to "Miss England", which achieved the world's water speed record at over 100 m.p.h.

Above: Small lathes used to machine general parts are shown behind a number of propellers awaiting despatch. *Left:* A view of the propeller grinding shop at John Street circa 1955 where propeller castings were measured and hand ground to produce an accurately finished propeller.

Memories of STOCKPORT

In 1944 Fred Bamford died and the Company passed into the hands of his son, also named Fred, who was a keen racer of boats and hydroplanes using, of course, Bamford propellers.

In 1947 Frank Smith, at the age of 25, the father of the current Managing Director, Andrew Smith, joined the Company as Assistant Managing Director and one year later, together with George Robinson, the Works Director, bought the company from Fred Bamford Junior.

During the fifties the Company continued to flourish with propellers and shafts being supplied world-wide to both commercial ships and navies. It also went back into marine engine production by marinising diesel engines under its trade name "Ajax" and manufacturing other products such as pumps and, more notably, flow switches. With this amount of activity, space was always a problem, the Company having premises dotted about all over Stockport with the John Street Works the main site but also with other operations at Charlesworth Street, Lee Street, Hanson Street and Warth Meadow. So, in 1959 a new factory was built at Whitehill to bring all the activities under one roof.

With more space, the size of the propellers and shafts increased with propellers as large as 4.2m and weighing five tonnes and shafts as long as 19m and weighing eleven tonnes.

In 1964 George Robinson died, Frank Smith bought his shares and the Smith family still run the Company which continues to specialise in the supply of long, thin and difficult propeller shafts together with specialist propellers for both military and civil applications. The flow switch business has also prospered and today supplies high quality flowmeters to many industries throughout the world.

Above: A 4.2 metre diameter propeller made at the Whitehill Street works in the mid 1960s. This is the largest controllable pitch propeller made by the company and was designed to drive a gravel dredger.

Right: The company's lorry shown at the rear of the John Street works circa 1957. The lorry is standing on Ridgeway Lane which is now covered by a car park and the Police Station. The lorry was unusually long for the time and was specially made by Leyland on a coach chassis for carrying marine propeller shafts like the one in the foreground.

Memories of STOCKPORT

Philips Semiconductors - from glass valves to the microchip.

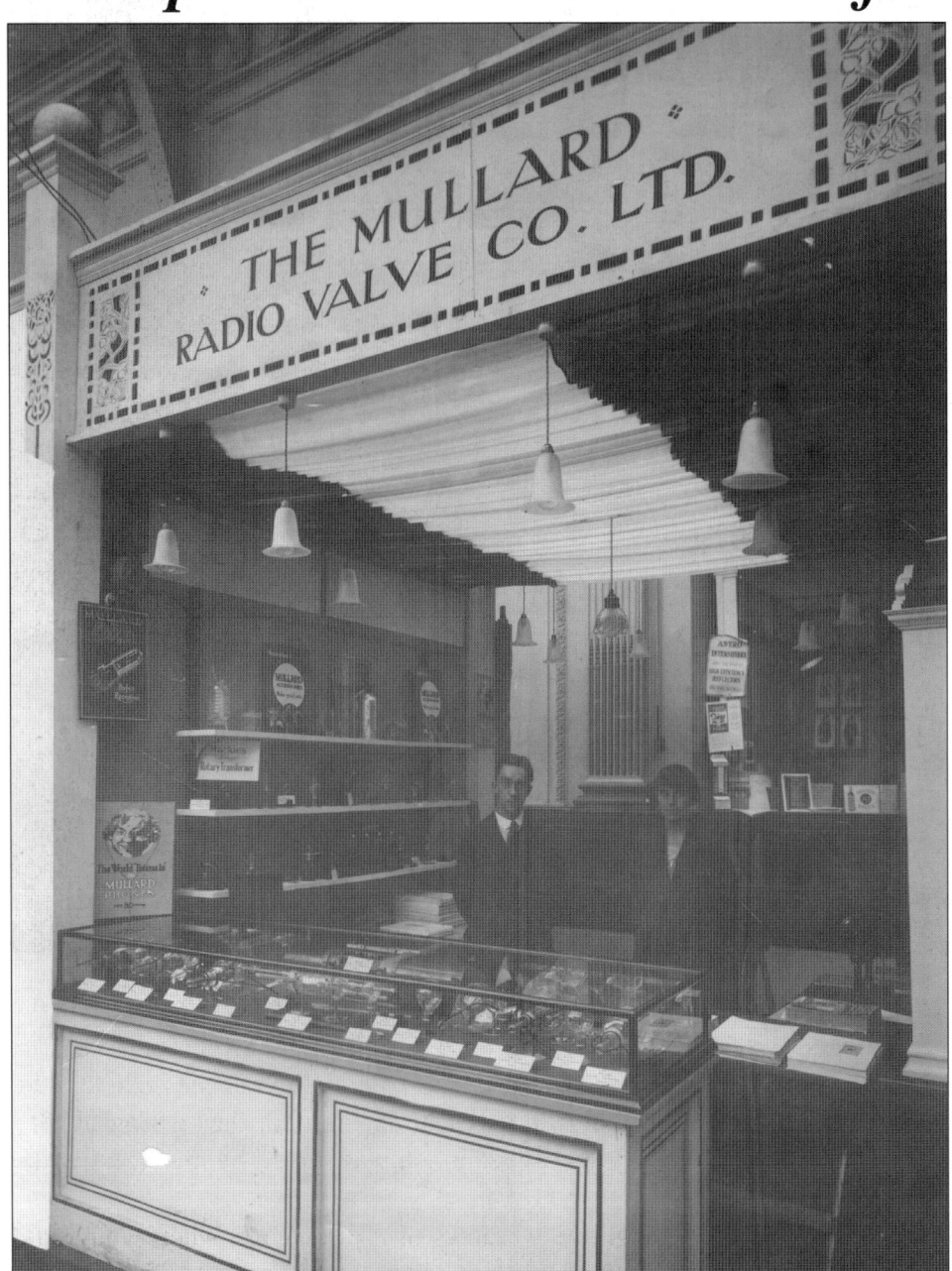

Philips Semiconductors, based in Hazel Grove, is justly proud of what it has achieved in Stockport and throughout the world. Whilst today it operates from modern premises producing sophisticated solid state devises, it had much humbler beginnings.

The company had its roots in what was a furniture factory in School Street, Hazel Grove. From Salford Electrical Instruments it later became part of GEC Semiconductors with additional premises in Broadstone Mill, Reddish.

In a joint venture between GEC and Mullards, the Company was established as Associated Semiconductor Manufacturers (ASM) in 1962, only to become solely owned by Mullards in 1969. 1970 saw the move to the present site just off Pepper Road in Hazel Grove.

Memories of STOCKPORT

It was not until 1988 that the name Philips Components was adopted to better reflect the move forwards from the making of valves to silicon chips. In recent years the name Philips Semiconductors placed the company firmly on the new technology map, making it a modern company, proud of its history and its present and confident with its people of a successful future.

Facing page, left picture: The whereabouts and exact date of this exhibition stand used to showcase Mullards radio valves is not known, but appears to be in the mid to late 1920s.

Facing page, right picture: These eight smartly uniformed "Mullard Boys" pose for another exhibition photograph, probably taken in the mid 1930s.

Above and Left: Many of the company's existing employees have been with the company since the days when it was based in the School Street factory. As the pictures on this page show, the girls sat shoulder-to-shoulder at benches which were polished every Friday. If one of the girls was getting married, they'd sing all day long. They would sing at Christmas too, when lunch was served by managers in the canteen.

Birds would regularly fly in through the windows of the canteen, where you could have bacon sandwiches and un-buttered toast, baked by an 80 year old canteen-lady.

Memories of STOCKPORT

W H Crossley, a Stockport family firm for over 175 years.

Seventeen years before the start of Queen Victoria's reign there was a tinsmith's shop on Castle Street, Edgeley. It was festooned with tin baths, buckets and other containers made in a small workshop at the back of the shop. The proprietor was William Henry Crossley, the first of six generations of Crossleys', still trading under his name, W. H. Crossley and Son Ltd., in Edgeley. That small workshop is now absorbed into twelve thousand square feet of premises on James Street and Worral Street. The shop itself was sold at auction at the Warren Bulkley Arms in 1922 for the then princely sum of £900.

The firm expanded under the direction of William's son Joseph and won many awards at national agricultural shows for its milk churns and other dairy equipment. Under the stewardship of the second William Henry Crossley came the advent of the motor car and Crossleys became one of the best known mudguard and panel manufacturers in the country establishing contracts with major motor manufacturers of the day. Amongst Crossleys' customers was the Ford Motor Company, who had a factory at Old Trafford making the Model T, and the Belsize motor company, who used Crossley panels and mudguards. A 1937 price list shows that Crossleys would supply front and rear mudguards for an Austin Seven for 15 shillings, that's 75 pence for those too young to remember "real" money.

Memories of STOCKPORT

With the move from hand built cars to production line manufacturing, fourth generation Joe and his son John took the firm into ducting for heating and ventilation applications and into pressed components, bracketry, control panels and boxes.

Jonathan and Dominic, sixth generation Crossleys, have extended the business further in to the exhibition, shop-fitting and display industries. In addition, sophisticated computer controlled machinery produces goods for industries as diverse as leisure and defence electronics, a far cry from gramophone horns made for HMV.

The company is rightly proud of its long history in Stockport and its tradition of combining modern methods with the craft skills of a loyal workforce and the directors and staff of Crossleys look forward to the millennium with optimism and an eagerness for the challenges ahead.

Facing page, main picture: William Henry Crossley's shop in Castle Street, Edgeley. The milk churns, buckets, watering cans and metal jugs were all hand made in the rear of the premises by the proprietor. *Facing page, far left:* William Crossley and his family, taken by a Victorian photographer of 26 Greek Street, Stockport. *Above:* A 1960s picture of Mr E Wilson and Mr K Riley working on a steel industrial camera case. *Right:* Joseph Crossley, son of the founder of the firm.

W H CROSSLEY & SON LIMITED   Est. 1820

For metal fabrications to customers specifications
Batch production of panels, brackets, boxes, guards, enclosures, cabinets etc. on CNC Punch and Brake Presses.

Worrall Street, Edgeley, Stockport, Cheshire SK3 9BE

Tel. 0161-480-2461
Fax 0161-474-7360

E.mail whc@crossley.u-net.com   Web site - http://www.high peaknet.com.crossley
Drawings can be accepted on floppy disk or down loaded in DXF format by modem.

Memories of STOCKPORT

McVitie's biscuits, baked in Stockport since 1917.

Today McVitie's is a household name, well known as the country's leading biscuit baker. For Stockport people the name also has a local significance, as the company has had an important presence since 1917, when the McVitie's biscuit factory first opened.

The McVitie's story begins in 1830, when Robert McVitie, an apprentice baker from Dumfries, moved to a tenement house at 150, Rose Street, Edinburgh. There, in the basement, the first McVitie's bakery was established. The business prospered and by the middle of the nineteenth century was firmly established as a high quality retail bakery and confectionery business.

Left: The despatch department of McVitie's Stockport factory on a typically busy 1950s day. *Below:* McVitie's Digestive has been with us for over 100 years. This charming period advertisement captures a 1930s family scene.

Memories of
STOCKPORT

The restrictions on supplies and transport that followed the Second World War led to negotiations being opened between the rival companies of McVitie & Price and MacFarlane Lang. The two companies successfully co-operated and this eventually resulted in the formation of United Biscuits in 1948.

The demand for quality biscuits saw production increase across the company and the Stockport bakery continued to play its part in meeting the increased sales demand. The factory started to make the Penguin biscuit which went on to become McVitie's most popular biscuit bar with sales of over £30 million per year. Today McVitie's is a British company employing over 7000 people throughout the UK. The Stockport factory has a workforce of approximately 900. The company prides itself on the skills of its staff, quality of its baking and ingredients and the innovation of its new product development which secures its 25% share of the £1.6 billion biscuit market.

Left: A 1960s picture of staff working on the Penguin line.
Below left: Two cheerful McVitie's staff packing Rich Tea biscuits. *Below:* A trilby hatted helper gets "hands-on" with a tanker delivery in this 1950s picture. All photographs were taken at the Stockport factory.

In 1888 Robert McVitie's baking skills were supplemented by Charles Price's selling expertise. This was so successful that Charles Price soon became a full partner and the firm became known as McVitie & Price. Charles Price was to work with McVitie for thirteen years until he left the firm in 1901 when he was elected a Liberal MP. Although the partnership was dissolved by mutual agreement, the name of McVitie & Price remained. By the First World War, McVitie & Price was called on by the Government to produce "iron ration" plain biscuits and to meet this demand the Stockport bakery was opened in 1917, which marked the beginning of an association with the town that has continued ever since.

Memories of STOCKPORT

Mirrlees Blackstone - from tank engines to power stations - all built in Stockport...

Mirrlees Blackstone, whose large site at Hazel Grove is a well known landmark in the area, has a history stretching back to 1840, when an engineering partnership was established in the Glasgow area to manufacture sugar cane processing machinery. But the Stockport connection actually began in 1906 when Charles Day, the Chairman of The Mirrlees Watson Company Limited, oversaw the construction of a factory at Hazel Grove. The company had by then become involved in the production of diesel engines, indeed the third diesel engine to be built anywhere in the world and the first in Britain had been made by the company in 1897.

By 1912 the patent that Mirrlees had taken out on the diesel engine expired, thus allowing competition into the industry, however the lead that Mirrlees had taken in the infancy of diesel engine production stood them in good stead and they became a market leader in the industry.

During the years of the Great War the Mirrlees factory developed a special diesel engine for use in what was then a new invention - the tank. The demands of war also meant that many women took the place of men in shop floor duties throughout 1914-18 conflict. The years between the First and Second World Wars saw the company develop new and more efficient diesel engines, becoming a major supplier to the admiralty, as well as many civil applications.

The dawning of war in 1939 saw Mirrlees swing over to defence production, with diverse projects providing power for radar installations, airfields, minesweepers and landing craft for the war effort. After the war, Mirrlees joined the Brush Group, which later became part of the Hawker Siddeley Group.

Today, Mirrlees Blackstone employs around 1000 people globally, is a world leader in the supply of diesel power for the production of electricity in island communities, mines, hospitals and ships etc.

Now part of the BTR Group, they maintain a philosophy which ensures that the most up-to-date methods of manufacture and training are adopted and with over 180 years of experience to draw from, confidently look forward to the next millennium.

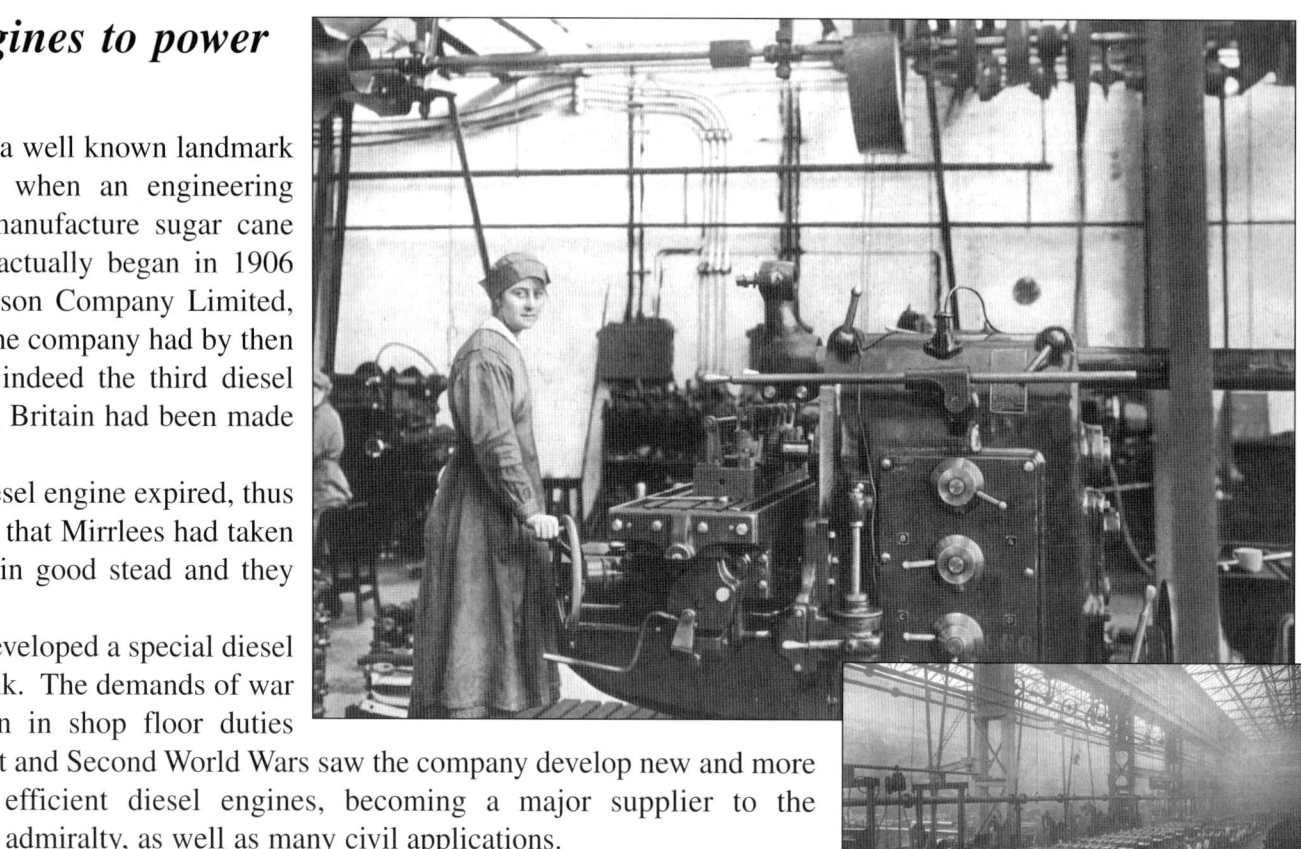

Left: The managers of the company in 1918.
Above (large picture): Women workers took the place of men during the First World War, when Mirrlees produced engines for tanks. *Above: (inset):* Rows of cylinder blocks for 250 bhp tank engines await assembly.

Changing face of the town centre

Right: One part of Stockport's landscape that has long since disappeared is Union Bridge, pictured here from both its ends. Union Bridge was a metal footbridge that spanned the Mersey, connecting the two parts of what was then called Union Road. The bridge provided access between Great Underbank (behind the photographer in this view) and Princes Street, which can just be made out in the distance.

Left: This view of Union Bridge dates from around the same year as that above - 1935. It is not too surprising that so many people appear to be looking over the side of the bridge at the activity below - this would have been an excellent vantage point to watch the work progressing on the building of Merseyway, which was a substantial civil engineering feat in its day.

Memories of
STOCKPORT

The building of Merseyway has been a major undertaking twice in the twentieth century history of Stockport. The first occasion was when the Mersey was culverted in order to create Merseyway - the road version (as opposed to the shopping centre, covered later in this book). This was done in two sections, the first was completed in 1934 and stretched from Wellington Road to Mersey Bridge, at a cost of £23,000. Sixty-two yards of the river were covered and Mersey Bridge altered to take the new road.

The section section of the new road began in 1936. Five hundred yards of the river were covered this time, from Mersey Bridge to Lancashire Bridge. These 1939 pictures shows the work progressing on the second section, with the rear of British Home Stores visible to the right.

Stockport Libraries

Memories of
STOCKPORT

Section two of Merseyway was completed in 1940 with the road officially opening on Monday September 30th, 1940. The total cost of this section was £109,000. This mid 1950s view shows a busy day for traffic on Merseyway, with an interesting collection of cars in the queue, including a Ford Consul with its "american" styling looking very modern alongside the Ford Pilot adjacent to it.

Interestingly, by using the position of the British Home Stores building as a reference point, this particular part of Merseyway can be seen on the page opposite in the early stages of construction.

After over 24 years as one of Stockport's main road thoroughfares, Merseyway began to be converted to one of the country's earlier pedestrianised shopping precincts, with the work taking a total of six years to complete.

Stockport Libraries

Memories of STOCKPORT

The last thirty years have seen some of the town centre areas of Stockport change almost beyond recognition, with other area swept away altogether. One of the former is Mersey Square, in many ways once the focal point of the town centre. The building of Merseyway in the 1930s resulted in the creation of a large volume of traffic, as this 1960 picture shows. The Mersey public house, since renamed the Chestergate Tavern, acts as a good reference point for this photograph and enables the reader to compare this picture with the much changed view today.

Memories of STOCKPORT

The concrete skeleton of the Merseyway shopping centre rises up in this 1968 picture. The whole Merseyway complex took six years to complete, with the final work finishing in 1970. The 1960s were a decade of change in many towns and cities across the country, when the post-war economic boom fuelled investment in new shopping centres, and the increase in motor car ownership dictated the need to provide more car parking spaces in central shopping areas. The Portwood cooling tower is visible through the mist of this November day.

Memories of STOCKPORT

Merseyway shopping centre viewed from The Bridge Restaurant in mid 1968, looking towards British Home Stores. Work was still progressing in other areas of Merseyway when this picture was taken, and there is evidence of the finishing touches still being carried out in this view. This picture looks decidedly modern and belies the fact that it is almost thirty years old. The clothes of the late 1960s shoppers provide the most obvious clue to its date.

Memories of
STOCKPORT

An aerial picture of the Portwood/Town Centre area taken in the mid 1970s. The River Goyt can just be made out in the top left of the picture adjacent to Millgate Power Station. Opened in 1898, the power station was coal fired until 1963 when it switched to oil fired in order to comply with the Clean Air Act, designed to reduce the rising levels of smog in may British towns and cities. Before the establishment of the national grid Stockport's electricity was generated by Millgate power station, although in its early years there was not much demand for electricity. Indeed, in 1904 just 217 customers had an electricity supply in a town with a population of 94,000. By the 1920s the demand for electricity and the appliances that were powered by it had increased so much that the corporation opened its first electricity showroom at 23 Tiviot Dale.

Memories of
STOCKPORT

A collection of views of Mersey Square cover this page and the one opposite, all taken in the early 1960s period. In this view The George public house stands in the top left hand corner of the picture, on the corner of Wellington Road North and Heaton Lane. The pub is still there today, although it is now dwarfed by office blocks immediately next to it. The inset picture shows the Fire Station and bus garage at Mersey Square, both of which were demolished to make way for the Merseyway shopping precinct.

Memories of
STOCKPORT

This view of Mersey Square dates from a similar date to the one opposite, but captures the area from a completely different angle. The Fire Station, Bus Garage and block of shops on the corner of Prince's Street were all casualties of the Merseyway redevelopment that was to be completed a decade after this picture was taken. The inset picture shows the Plaza Cinema in the mid distance, one of the relatively few buildings to survive in Mersey Square.

Memories of STOCKPORT

This particular view of Mersey Square is one that shows less change than some of the other views of this part of town. The Mersey public house is still there, although renamed as the Chestergate Tavern, and Rock Row has survived relatively unscathed. Buses don't look like that anymore, though!

Memories of STOCKPORT

Work on the new Merseyway shopping precinct was well under way when this 1967 photograph was taken. The planning process for Merseyway had taken many years from the original idea to the plans being agreed by the corporation, and the building work itself then took six years to complete, so it was with some relief that the work was completed in 1970.

Memories of STOCKPORT

Left: An early 1960s view of the edge of the Market Place, with the Millgate power station cooling tower looming large in the background.

Below left: The imposing frontage of the Stockport Co-operative Society's *New Central Emporium* makes an impressive sight in this picture from 1947.

Below: The Plaza Cinema in Mersey Square is one of the few buildings in that area to survive the changes of the last sixty years. The Plaza opened in 1932, around when this picture was taken, and by 1946 it was one of the 18 cinemas in Stockport. In those pre-television days cinema was a major part of family entertainment, as well as being a way of keeping up with world events through newsreels. But the popularity of the small screen was to eventually take its toll and the Plaza now serves as a bingo hall.

At war

Edgeley Station, 1939, and the storm clouds of war were gathering over Europe. The Sixth Battalion of the Cheshire Regiment can be seen proudly marching through the station, accompanied by a collection of excited children. Little did these people know that six years of war were to follow, with hundreds of thousands of British servicemen and women losing their lives, along with thousands of civilians. Indeed the year after this picture was taken bombs fell on Stockport, bringing death and mayhem to the town's streets.

Memories of STOCKPORT

Left: The first bomb raid to hit Stockport was on October 2nd 1940, when eight high explosive bombs and a number of incendiary devices fell in Portwood, Hillgate, Cheadle Heath and Heaton Moor. Marsland Street took the worst hit, four people were killed and dozens of houses were either flattened or rendered unsafe.

The street pictured on the left, Montagu Road in Offerton, shows the aftermath of a 1940 bomb raid. At the time this picture was taken these houses were only a few years old and had been built in the inter-war period of growth in suburban houses. Then, semi-detached houses were a relatively new phenomenon, and would have cost their first owners around £400, with a deposit of £22 and repayments of 14 shillings. Virtually all of the houses in the picture were saved and still stand today.

Right: With war on the horizon in 1938, Stockport corporation took the decision to provide large scale air-raid shelters in the centre of the town. As a result, engineers were commissioned to enlarge an existing series of tunnels, which were eventually to form an inter-connecting network in Portwood, Brinksway and Lancashire Hill. Building work took four years, finishing in 1942. This view shows the Highbankside entrance to the tunnels, which were capable of providing refuge for up to 5,000 people.

Memories of STOCKPORT

A Stockport street party in August 1945. VE day brought immense relief to families throughout Britain, with the end of hostilities in Europe meaning that husbands, brothers and sons could return to the family. On the home front, women had not only kept house and home in order, but had been the major force behind the wheels of industry, working on the shop floor in many local factories. The "V for Victory" sign, made famous by Churchill, is much in evidence in this happy scene.

Stockport Libraries

The Stockport air disaster

Sunday June 4th, 1967 began like any other Sunday in Stockport. At just after 10.00 am most people were going about their usual Sunday morning business, when the sound of an aeroplane flying overhead broke the peace. But this was not the usual sound of an aircraft on its descent into Ringway airport, the noise was louder and the height of the plane, an Argonaut airliner carrying 84 passengers and crew, was alarmingly low. A petrol station attendant in Portwood was later to say that he thought the plane would crash straight into the cooling tower.

Memories of STOCKPORT

The stricken craft, owned by British Midland Aviation and on its return flight from Palma, Majorca, was losing height by the second and the pilot decided to put the plane down on the only tiny pocket of open land in the centre of Stockport. In the enquiry that was to follow, Captain Harry Marlow, aged 41, was praised for avoiding the many heavily occupied buildings that surrounded Hopes Carr, where the plane was to crash land at 10.10 am.

The plane split into three sections on landing, and destroyed an electricity sub-station, cutting off 750 households. Within minutes dozens of locals were on the scene helping to pull people from the wreckage, using only their bare hands.

But for the fire that followed, many more people might have survived, but tragically 72 of those on board the aircraft lost their lives. Mercifully, there were no casualties on the ground. Captain Marlow and one of the stewardesses were among the twelve survivors. The relatives of the passengers who were awaiting the arrival of the plane at Ringway were gathered together in a private lounge and informed of the tragedy by the airport's director, Mr George Harvey. The enquiry into the tragedy reported in August 1968, when the cause of the crash was linked to a serious fuel problem resulting in the loss of two of the planes four engines.

Captain Marlow suffered serious head injuries in the crash which meant he had to leave his job. He was later to buy a launderette in the Midlands, which he ran with his wife, Bobbie.

Football memories

After an eleven year absence, Stockport County made a welcome return to Division Two as Champions of the Northern section of Division Three. In the final game of the season, an Edgeley Park crowd of 26,135 saw County win the title with a 2-0 win over runners-up Lincoln City. Joe Hill, who finished the club's top scorer with 21 goals and a George Stevens penalty ensured The Championship success.

The club were rewarded with a celebration dinner which was held at Stockport Town Hall on Tuesday 25th May, 1937. The characatures were drawn on the reverse of the menu by local sports writer Tom Turton. The two players, captured as drawings on the menu (see left), were Billy Bocking and Frank McDonough and were both huge personalities of the day.

Memories of STOCKPORT

Despite being 32 years of age when he signed for Stockport County in October 1951, Jack Connor was to write himself into the club's record books thanks to a strike rate of two goals every three games from his five seasons stay, his 140 league and cup goals from just 217 games, set a record that remains intact to the present day.

His travels had seen him play in Scotland with albion Rovers and Ireland with Ards. After spells with several English clubs, Jack went to Bradford City. It was whilst he was playing there that he was tracked down to a Bradford cinema, signing up there and then to play for County for a fee of £2,500. He still lives locally and is seen above scoring County's second goal against Workington in the club's 2-0 victory at Edgeley Park on October 10th, 1953.

Memories of
STOCKPORT

The arrival of manager Jimmy Meadows was to signal a change in County's fortunes after finishing just 13th in the previous term. Changes were made in the playing staff, with the former Blackburn Rovers centre-half, Matt Woods, installed as Captain and Eddie Stuart, the former Wolves star, joining in defence. Five victories from the opening six games set the pace with the Championship being wrapped up by the time that Lincoln City spoiled the party with a 5-4 win in the final match of the campaign. **Pictured above:** Captain Matt Woods is hoisted shoulder high with the 4th Division Championship Trophy in front of the main stand at Edgeley Park, before County's last game of the successful 1966-67 season.

Gone shopping!

There has been a market in Stockport on or near to the present site for the last 700 years, and the present cast-iron and glass covered Market Hall dates from 1861. The Market Hall itself was modified in 1912 when a section was removed to enable the passage of a trolley bus route through the Market Place. The picture above shows the West side of the Market in 1949. In the immediate post-war period money was very tight and rationing still in place for many household items, however, the Market was still a busy place, with bargains to be had on every stall, just like today!

Memories of
STOCKPORT

As well as housing a vibrant market, the Market Place is also home to some interesting buildings, many of which can be seen in this 1961 view. The building on this side of the mock-tudor frontage served as a pub from 1824 until 1951, called The Angel. The former Produce Market is also visible on the far right of the picture, with its four "Corinthian" columns. It was initially constructed as a single storey building in 1852, with the upper section added in 1875 to house the Free Library. The old-style telephone boxes add to the nostalgic feel of this busy market scene.

Memories of
STOCKPORT

The original Co-operative premises on Chestergate were built in 1925 and named "The Fashion House". In the 1930s expansion led to the development of the building and in 1937 the extended and refurbished premises were opened. The renamed Co-operative Central Emporium boasted a 215 feet extension along Chestergate, with a central block and two wings, with the original building forming one of the wings. Merseyway was in the process of being built at the time and this was borne in mind with the new building, with provision for an arcade opening onto the Merseyway side in the new design. Surprisingly, both the architects and the building contractors for the Co-operative Emporium were in-house departments of the Stockport Industrial and Equitable Co-operative Society Limited.

Memories of STOCKPORT

Left: The provisions counter in the Food Hall of the new Co-operative Central Emporium is displayed in this picture, like the other on this page reproduced from the store's 1937 brochure. The counters were fitted with "Vitrolite" fronts and stainless steel fittings. The Food Hall also housed Grocery, Confectionery, Cooked Meats and the Greengrocery departments, with a Tobacco Kiosk which was also accessible from the street.

Right: The basement of the new building housed the Crockery, Wireless, Electrical Goods, Wallpaper, Paints, Sports Equipment and (pictured) the Hardware departments, as well as a Milk Bar. The basement space in the old building was occupied by the Heavy Drapery department. The fittings on the basement floor were constructed in Austrian Oak with veneers of Austrian Walnut laid in. The displays were said at the time to be the latest word in design, with careful use of lighting to display the goods to their best effect.

The Co-operative Emporium was to serve Stockport shoppers for generations and these pictures of the "new" interior layout as it was in 1937 will, doubtless, bring back memories for many who have visited it since then.

Memories of STOCKPORT

Little Underbank is undoubtedly one of Stockport's more charismatic streets, with fine arcitechture. This picture dates from circa 1955, and contains at least two popular landmarks, both of which survive to this day. One of them is Winter's clock, visible above the opticians and jewellers of that name. The gold leaf lettering is also still present, although the premises now house a bistro/winebar. Petersgate Bridge makes another good reference piont, with the Queens Head, also known as "Turner's Vaults", just past the bridge on the left. Judging by the heavy coats and scarves being worn, this was a cold day, probably in late autumn or early winter...brrrrrr!

Memories of STOCKPORT

Ernest Axon, a pioneer of the building industry in Stockport.

Over the past few years the construction industry, along with many others, has suffered from the difficult economical climate so it is hard to imagine that Ernest Axon Ltd is 125 years old this year. Also when one considers the last 125 years it is quite an achievement that any company should still be owned and run by the same family.

The founder was Thomas Axon who had two sons, Ernest and Thomas. The photograph (above) is Ernest Axon. Ernest ran the builders merchants whilst Thomas was a flag-pole and ladder maker. Both businesses ran side by side and continued to do so after their father's death.

Records show that the business started in 1871 at Baker Street, Heaton Norris in the names of William and Thomas Axon 'Lathrenders'.

In the 1880's the business moved again, this time to Laurel Street, Heaton Norris. The offices were run from Laurel Street right until the 1960's.

After Thomas' death, Ernest took over the running of the business in Laurel Street, operating under the name of Ernest Axon & Co. It was only in July 1930 that the business was incorporated as Ernest Axon Limited. He continued as Managing Director until his death in 1941 at the age of 61. He was a prominent and well respected figure in the town at the time, serving on the Town Council for many years.

Memories of STOCKPORT

Main picture, opposite page: Wellington Road North can be seen stretching away into the distance in this view, dating from the early 1960s. Ernest Axon's premises can be made out in the centre of the picture, next to the chimney and church spire. This area is now occupied by the Inland Revenue Offices.

This page, far left: Ernest Axon (on the left) stands proudly next to one of their firm's lorries at the Stockport Carnival in 1938.

Left: The Directors of Ernest Axon Limited, (left to right) Paul, Susan and Tony Buckley.

Before the outbreak of the Second World War the founder's grandson, also called Ernest, joined the business at the age of fourteen. He helped the drivers with their deliveries until he could learn to drive himself. Ernest was eventually called up for the army, serving in North Africa and Italy, and reaching the rank of sergeant before the end of the war.

In 1985 Ernest decided it was time to retire, having seen the business move from strength to strength. During his 50 years in the business he had witnessed all kinds of changes to the building industry but he was confident to leave the company in the capable hands of his daughter, son-in-law and now his grandson. With the millenium on the horizon, the company's aim is to continue to give the same level of service to the building trade and to hope that there will be another generation of the Axon family at the helm.

ERNEST AXON LIMITED
BUILDERS MERCHANTS STOCKPORT

Suppliers to the building trade for 125 years and still a family business 1871-1996

Tel: 0161 428 0314
Fax: 0161 491 0844

Unit 1, McKenzie Industrial Park, Bird Hall Lane, Cheadle Heath, Stockport, SK3 0SB

Memories of STOCKPORT

Alfred and Maurice Matlow started Matlow Bros. Ltd. in a small factory in London in 1928 after having previously gained both practical and technical experience within the confectionery industry. Production was originally confined to the manufacture of Table jellies and Jelly type confectionery but today embraces Boiled Sweets in bags and tins, toffees, eclairs, chews, bubble gum, sugar free sweets, marshmallow, sugar coated products, puffed cereal lines, gums and chocolate coated nuts.

In 1933 the two brothers together with David Dee formed Swizzels Ltd, commencing in factory premises at Star Lane, Canning Town, London E16 and in the same year moved to larger premises in Drivers Avenue, Plaistow, London.

Swizzels Ltd specialised in the manufacture of fizzy sweets in compressed tablet form, an idea that subsequently developed into the present day nationally known range of Love Hearts, Sherbits, Fruit Fizzers, Double Lollies, Parma Violets, Refreshers and Navy Mints. In 1940 both companies, having been subjected to the effects of the 'blitz' evacuated to a disused textile mill in New Mills, Derbyshire. The Mill, now nearly 150 years old, was rebuilt during 1883 due to a fire and is now largely used for offices and stores.

Steady developments of business, both at home and abroad, called for considerable expansion of both production and warehouse facilities.

In 1971 a new factory extension was opened on the same site, providing an additional 107,000 sq. ft. of floor area. At the same time completely new plants for fully automated manufacture were installed.

1971 was in fact an eventful year for Swizzels Matlow, as Swizzels Ltd was awarded the Queens Award to Industry for export achievement.

In fact nearly half of their products are exported to more than 40 countries throughout the world.

Towards the end of 1974 a further 7000 sq. ft. of production warehousing was added and a factory extension of 40,000 sq. ft. was completed in 1978. In 1976, 85,000 sq. ft. of production and warehouse space was obtained when the old Paper Mill, known as Grove Mill, was bought.

In 1975 the company adopted the title of Swizzels Matlow Limited to symbolise the complete integration of the two companies.

Swizzels Matlow are the largest employer in the New Mills area, having a work force of over 600.

Above: A Swizzels lorry takes part in a local gala procession during the late 1940s.

This advert dates from 1965

Memories of STOCKPORT

Part of the Swizzels fleet in the 1950s. The company's vans have always been excellent mobile advertising boards.

A Matlow Brothers exhibition stand - possibly at Olympia in the 1930s.

The company is still essentially a family concern, the joint Chairmen being Mr David Dee and Mr Maurice Matlow. The sons of the founders are all actively involved as Directors of the company and have now been joined by the third generation. Their functions are by no means rigidly defined and perhaps the secret of the success of the company can be attributed to their versatility.

Swizzels Matlow are particularly fortunate in still having a number of employees with a life time of service with the company.

Swizzels Matlow are still best known for the products which have been household names for years, i.e. Love Hearts, Refreshers, Fizzers, Double Lollies, Chews, Rainbow Drops, New Refreshers, Drumstick Lollies, bettabars and travel tins to name a few.

For the more adult tastes, Matlow's Milk and Plain Chocolate Brazils have a ready market. In 1984 the company was honoured to receive from the British Safety Council, the 'Sword of Honour', being one of only 30 companies throughout the whole world to receive the award for having a lower accident record than any other company in their industry. They were also honoured to receive the 'Fit for Work' Award in 1986 for outstanding achievement in the employment of disabled people.

Memories of STOCKPORT

Chestergate Wood Supplies Ltd. - one of Stockport's small business successes.

Stockport has bred many business success stories, and undoubtedly one of them is Chestergate Wood Supplies Ltd., which is based at Borron Street, just off Great Portwood Street. The business began in a humble fashion when, in 1961, Mr. C.M. Jennings set up a small shop hardly larger than the average living room on the corner of King Street and Chestergate, hence the name of the business.

The keen prices and efficient service soon saw the business prosper and grow, with personal recommendation bringing a steady stream of new customers.

By 1971, the stock carried by the business had expanded substantially, with what was then a relatively new concept - D.I.Y, accounting for much of the firm's trade. The original premises were no longer large enough to accommodate the company, and so the search for more a suitable base began.

The result was Mr. Jennings moved the business to the large, airy industrial unit of 5000 square feet which the company still occupies to this day. A measure of the D.I.Y skills of Chestergate staff was that the new premises were entirely fitted out by the company's own staff, who at that time numbered seven.

Above and facing page: The original premises on the corner of King Street and Chestergate are captured in this late sixties scene, shortly before Chestergate Wood supplies moved to their new premises in Borron Street.

Memories of STOCKPORT

Self-selection was quite a new idea back in 1971, but the new premises offered this convenient way of purchasing from day one.

The store is now run by the second generation of the Jennings family in the form of Michael Jennings, who has been involved in the business since leaving school and has kept the traditions and high standards of value and customer service set by his father.

In these days of national multiple chains it is heartening to see a local, long established business prospering by offering choice, value and service. After three decades of trading in Stockport the business is still going from strength to strength, and the staff and management look forward to the next thirty years with confidence.

A FAMILY BUSINESS FOR OVER 35 YEARS!

SUPPLIERS TO:
DIY ENTHUSIASTS
HOME IMPROVERS
TRADE CUSTOMERS
LARGE COMPANIES
LOCAL AUTHORITIES
SCHOOLS
COLLEGES
HEALTH AUTHORITIES
LOCAL COMPANIES
MULTI-NATIONAL COMPANIES

Mr Chippie, as he looked in 1961, alongside today's version.

HOURS:
MON, WED, THUR 8.30-6pm
TUES 9.00-6pm
FRI (late night) 8.30-7.30pm
SAT 9.00-5pm
SUN. 10-4pm

☎ 0161-480 7138

CHESTERGATE
WOOD SUPPLIES LTD
BORRON ST. PORTWOOD STOCKPORT SK1 2JD

Memories of STOCKPORT

Anderson Motors, over forty years of service to Stockport motorists.

In today's bustling world of constant change and speed, the car business is a tough and very competitive challenge. Success here demands a keen mind, quick to seize every opportunity, a determination to keep going at all costs, a thorough knowledge of all aspects of the business, especially the technical side and a dedication to personal service. For the past forty years Bill Anderson has been building his business on these principles. The confidence of his customers and the overflowing order books are a fair measure of how he has succeeded.

The year was 1956. William R. Anderson, armed with a diploma in Automobile Engineering and his own personal skills decided to enter the world of business. What he lacked in experience Bill Anderson made up for in determination to succeed and a willingness to work hard.

He purchased premises at Buxton Road, Great Moor, Stockport and planned a modern, efficient garage which set new standards for sales and service. This was exceedingly ambitious but for Bill it was the final goal towards which every single step, plan and forecast was directed.

Andersons Buxton Road premises in the late 1960s

The first five years were sheer toil and sweat, long hours in the service of every customer but slowly the Anderson reputation took shape and the name became synonymous with expertise in tuning two stroke engines. This reputation played a big part when, in 1960, Saab were about to appoint distributors in the North West. Anderson Motors Limited were the obvious choice.

With Saab the company took on new dimensions. Years of hard work continued but with more tangible results. A dealer network was built to support the distributorship, the spares department was greatly improved and there was an increased capacity for stocks. Servicing facilities were extended to meet the needs of the ever growing number of Saab owners in the North West. Special sales staff were employed, although the company policy was, and still is, 'a satisfied customer is the best salesman'. By the mid 60's it was obvious that the increase in business meant new premises were needed. It was decided that purpose built premises would be constructed on a local trading estate. A complete new garage was out of the question so the new premises were confined to Stores, Body Shop and New Vehicle Distribution facilities. The garage at Great Moor was extended at the same time. The service area increased and a new showroom and offices were added.

Considerable change has taken place since those earlier days. In 1973 Andersons moved to their present location at Buxton Road, Hazel Grove, Stockport, another step to improving customer service.

Andersons for the Saab of your choice.

To be the leading SAAB dealer in Cheshire and intending to keep it that way means that customer service is our number one priority. Whether you are buying a top of the range brand new SAAB or a bulb you will be treated with the same courtesy. Over the last forty years we have built our business on ensuring that our customers receive the service expected from a company selling up-market vehicles to a select clientele. The range of SAAB cars now available meets every criterion, but the choice is wide with the highest of specifications together with a whole host of options.

There is always a wide selection of new and used SAAB cars to choose from at our Hazel Grove showroom and you are more than welcome to browse at your leisure. There is no pressure selling at Anderson Motors, just helpful advice should you require it.

Our after sales is second to none, from parts to servicing your every need is catered for. So, if you are looking for that VIP treatment look no further than Anderson Motors, you know it makes sense.

Andersons

31 BUXTON ROAD, HAZEL GROVE, STOCKPORT,
CHESHIRE SK7 6AQ

Tel: 0161 483 6271

ANDERSONS MOTORS LTD
1956 — 40th ANNIVERSARY — 1996
STOCKPORT

SAAB SCANIA — SAAB

Memories of STOCKPORT

The Alma Lodge Hotel, a hostelry with history....

Since its humble beginnings the Jarvis Alma Lodge Hotel has grown in reputation and capacity to become Stockport's premier hotel and one of the most popular and respected hotels in the North West.

Ancient deeds show that the hotel was originally a farmhouse when Stockport was just a rural area. Stagecoaches used to pass along what is now known as Buxton Road as they made their way to and from London. As the surrounding area developed, the farmhouse was rebuilt and became a nine bedroom residence. It was only after the First World War that the house was bought and then transformed into a hotel.

Legend has it that in 1951 a group of local businessmen, which included Mr Reg Whalley, who was the owner of the Stockport Express, were chatting away after a 'hard day's golf' when one of them happened to mention that the hotel was for sale. Apparently that same afternoon, Mr Whalley bought the hotel and was installed as Chairman of the Board of Directors of the Alma Lodge Hotel Ltd.

The hotel was to never look back.

The Hotel remained under the ownership of Mr Whalley until the 1960s. During that time the Hotel was extended, modernised and had the Regis Suite added to it as well as other banqueting and conferencing facilities.

The Hotel has had its fair share of famous visitors. Former Prime Minister Harold McMillan stayed and was quoted as saying "After a very full day in Lancashire and Cheshire, my wife and I were very grateful to be able to spend a little time at the Alma Lodge Hotel. The arrangements were excellent and we could not have been looked after better by your staff. Please give them our thanks".

The hotel has been more recently visited by the Rt. Hon. John Major MP during the time of his Premiership.

Today the Alma Lodge is part of the Jarvis hotel group and has lost none of its charm and elegance. Indeed its traditions have been built on and it truly is a hotel that can offer all the modern services in a unique stylish environment.

The Hotel continues to modernise and improve its service. It can boast 52 en-suite bedrooms, a superb restaurant and conferencing facilities which can cater for up to 200 people with ease. The Jarvis Alma Lodge is certainly a hotel with a mood of its own and has a future that looks just as rosy as its colourful past.

Above: An early 1960s view of the Alma Lodge Hotel. The car park contains a collection of motor cars, including such great British names as Jaguar, Morris and Rover.

The Jarvis Alma Lodge Hotel

memorably traditional

How refreshing it is to find a hotel that prides itself on it's natural charm and elegance. Stepping into the Jarvis Alma Lodge Hotel is like being taken back in time. A carefully carved interior adorns the reception area and the whole mood is traditional.

The hotel has 52 en-suite bedrooms, Carvery Restaurant, and Cocktail bar. Each room has satellite TV, direct dial telephone and tea and coffee making facilities.

So, If your looking for a top class hotel with all the charm and elegance of a bygone era, look no further than the Jarvis Alma Lodge - Stockports finest Hotel.

For further details contact:

Jarvis Alma Lodge Hotel

149 Buxton Road · Heaviley · Stockport SK2 6EL · Telephone: 0161 483 4431

FOR A LONG TIME PART OF THE MEMORIES – AND PLANNING FOR THE FUTURE.

Stockport College have memories of thousands of exam successes and personal triumphs going back to the 1880s. Here in the 1990s our personal, caring teaching methods and facilities befitting one of the biggest colleges in the country are keeping us well suited to continue bringing tremendous benefits to the students of today and those of the future.

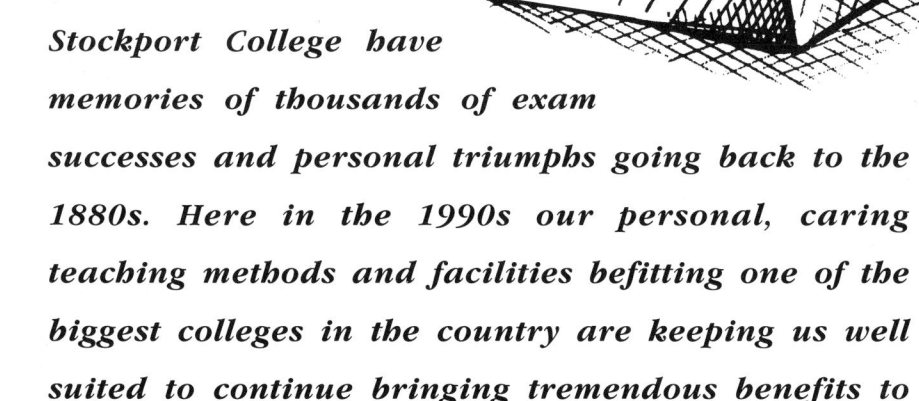

Study levels:

Basic skills, GCSEs, A Levels, Revision courses, Access to Higher Education, BTEC, GNVQs, NVQs, Craft Certificates, Professional Qualifications, Degrees.

Students:

School leaving age to retirement and beyond

Amenities include:

Information Technology Centre, sports halls, gymnasium, fitness testing centre, student's union, hairdressing and beauty salons, travel agency, shop, fast food restaurants, library with 75,000 books...

How to start:

First telephone **0161 958 3100** for a prospectus.

STOCKPORT *college*
OF FURTHER & HIGHER EDUCATION

Providing excellence in education and training

Memories of STOCKPORT

Stockport College - established 1889.

Stockport College of Further & Higher Education and its predecessors have figured in people's memories of Stockport since as long ago as 1886. In that year Sir Joseph Leigh, who was to be four times Mayor of Stockport, mooted the idea of a Technical School to celebrate the Golden Jubilee of Queen Victoria.

The local textile industry was suffering severe competition from abroad and there was an urgent need to train workers in new technology. Additionally, better facilities were being sought for training artists and craftsmen in the applied arts, particularly textile design and production.

A fund was established to finance the building of a combined Technical and Art School on part of the site of the present college. Sir Joseph Leigh, one of the sponsors of the Manchester Ship Canal, was a major subscriber and a £10,000 donation from Sir Joseph Whitworth's Residuary Legatees was to be divided equally between the building fund and the establishment of Whitworth Scholarships. The government's Department of Science and Art also made a substantial grant towards the establishment of the Art School.

When the old school opened in 1889 the automobile was only five years old, steam locomotion reigned supreme, the Wright Brothers would not fly for another fourteen years and a public electricity supply for Stockport was still at the planning stage. Nevertheless, the first 1,000 students enrolled for day and evening classes and had a wide choice of technical, scientific, commercial, artistic, academic and domestic science subjects which laid the foundation for today's very wide selection of courses in the same categories.

The college of today is notable for the wide range of study levels for students from school age right up to retirement age and beyond. The College is a University College of the University of Manchester.

Above and right: Students of the college shown in the laboratory setting from the 1920s and a woodwork lesson from around the turn of the century

Memories of STOCKPORT

The photographer who took this panorama almost certainly gained this semi-aerial view by taking the shot from one of the flats on King Street West. The picture dates from 1965 and shows the railway sidings next to what is now Stockport's main railway station.

Memories of STOCKPORT

STOCKPORT GRAMMAR SCHOOL

Leading HMC Independent School offering excellence in every aspect of education for boys and girls aged 4 - 18

Entry into the Junior School from age 4 is by application to the Junior School Headmaster.
Tel: 0161 419 2405

Entry into the Senior School from age 11 or into the sixth form is by application to the Headmaster's Secretary.
Tel: 0161 456 9000

**BUXTON ROAD,
STOCKPORT SK2 7AF
TEL: 0161 456 9000**
www.argonet.co.uk/users/sgs

STOCKPORT GRAMMAR SCHOOL IS A REGISTERED CHARITY NO 525936

He Who Endures Conquers

The founder of Stockport Grammar School, Sir Edmund Shaa, was born in Stockport and by 1448 was 200th Lord Mayor of London and Court Jeweller to three Kings of England. Sir Edmund's will directed that a "connying Preest kepe a gram scole contynually in the said Town of Stopforde".

Columbus had not discovered America when the first classes began in 1487 at St Mary's Church in Stockport but the School migrated twice from there before establishing itself in 1916 in the present buildings at Mile End. The climax of sixty years of expansion came in 1979 when the adjoining convent school was purchased. Girls were admitted in 1980 and the Senior School now numbers over 1000 pupils with a Junior School of over 300. A Direct Grant School until 1976, the school then reverted to independent status and now enjoys a national reputation for academic excellence and achievement.

Stockport Grammar School is proud of its long association with the town and the generations of local children educated there from every kind of background. The Mayor of Stockport is an ex-officio member of the Governing Body and the Governors themselves retain strong links with Stockport.

Notable pupils have been Admiral Back (the Arctic explorer), Professor Sir Frederick Williams (inventor of the stored computer programme) and the mountaineer Peter Boardman. Perhaps the most remarkable was John Bradshaw, who condemned Charles I to death and became the only Head of a truly Republican State in English history.

For the famous and the not so famous, Stockport Grammar School has remained dedicated to offering the finest education to all who can benefit, true to the wishes of its founders.

Memories of STOCKPORT

Simon-Carves, Over a century of achievement at home and overseas.

The story of Simon-Carves begins in the reign of Queen Victoria when the foundations were being laid for the highly technical world of today.

Henry Simon came to England in 1860 as a refugee from Prussian oppression and within a few years had established himself as a consulting engineer in Manchester. He then teamed up with Francois Carvès, a distinguished French coke oven engineer, to pioneer the by-product coke oven to replace the old beehive oven which wasted the volatile products of coal. The partnership led to the founding of Simon-Carves in 1880, and by 1882 the first British by-product coke ovens has been built and installed for Pease Partners at Crook, Co. Durham.

By the turn of the century Simon-Carves had become a leading British company in its field, and when a strong demand for Sulphuric acid arose during World War One a chemical plant department was formed to cater for this need. During the 1920's and 1930's an increasing reputation was gained for designing and building coke ovens and all manner of chemical plants. By the 1950's the company had developed extensive activities both at home and overseas, extending its chemical operations to include gasification, fertiliser, petroleum refining and petrochemical plants.

In 1960 a newly formed holding company, Simon Engineering Ltd., brought together Simon-Carves Ltd. and the flour milling and food engineering interests of Henry Simon Ltd., along with their many subsidiary and overseas companies. Simon-Carves continued to head the contracting side of business, and by the 1970's had acquired considerable expertise in a range of chemical, petrochemical, materials handling and industrial process plants. A particular success story concerned Simon-Carves' association with ICI in more than 30 contracts for the supply of high pressure polyethylene plants in 16 countries.

As the 21st century approaches, Simon-Carves maintains its strong position as an international contractor, pioneering new methods for designing and supplying plants of a complex nature to the world's chemical, food, nuclear and pharmaceutical industries

Above: The Simon-Carves purpose built offices and development laboratories at Cheadle Heath. *Left:* The Simon Carves by-product coking oven. The first in Britain, 1881, Co. Durham.

SIMON-CARVES LTD., SIM-CHEM HOUSE, PO BOX 17, CHEADLE HULME, CHEADLE, CHESHIRE SK8 5BR
TEL: 0161 485 6131 FAX: 0161 486 1302

Memories of STOCKPORT

The visit of the Queen Mother in the summer of 1960 saw local people lining the streets of the town centre. This picture captures an exclusively female crowd, excitedly gathered together in their best summer outfits. Pullars of Perth, the dry cleaning specialists are a name from High Streets of yesteryear and the ornate shopfront belonging to George Whitehead Stationers certainly belong to a previous era.

Memories of STOCKPORT

Friendly comradeship and mutual help

The Shepherds Friendly Society was founded on Christmas day 1826 at the Friendship Inn, Ashton under Lyne. Regular attenders had become conscious of the need to provide against poverty and the workhouse in time of illness. The Friendly Society Lodge was established on the principle of mutual self-help and protection. There were 12 original signatories known as The Founders whose original purpose was to relieve the sick and bury the dead. Regarded as the chief over these was a Mr Thomas Scholfield. By the time he died in 1870 the original promoters had grown into a membership of 40,000.

Lodges began to multiply, the first new one opening in 1827 at Mossley. Soon, as the movement spread through Lancashire and Yorkshire, it was decided to form separate districts with each group of lodges in an area having self-rule. By the 1860s it had become clear that the Society's financial basis was insecure and

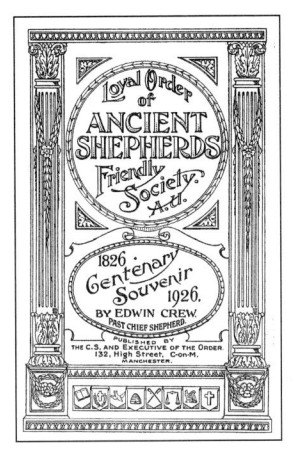

Memories of STOCKPORT

so a 'Great Reform' followed. A graduated scale of payments was introduced, depending on the age of prospective members. Not surprisingly there was some opposition from older members.

In 1891, proposed by the Greenock group, it became standard to establish a permanent funeral fund.

As financial arrangements became more satisfactorily settled, a policy of 'good works' was established and the first of these was the presentation of a lifeboat to the City of Bristol. Later, during the second war, lodges funded canteens and ambulances.

At the annual conference in Swansea in 1927 the Individual Account was inaugurated. There was criticism from those who pinned their faith wholly on the mutual policy but it was accepted by the majority.

Clients' contributions have been wisely invested throughout the Society's history so that its basis is financially secure. Then, in 1946, the government passed the National Insurance Act and the Friendly Societies lost state insurance business. These were worrying times of declining membership

However, a new head office was acquired in Manchester in 1951 and by 1955 new government legislation extended the power of Friendly Societies. In 1959 the National Insurance Bill increased state retirement pensions from increased compulsory contributions

The Head Office in Stockport was opened in July 1968 by the Chief Shepherd, John Campbell. The premises were very compact and lent themselves to efficient administration.

Today The Society offers life assurance, sickness benefits, savings' schemes and personal pension plans. Nevertheless, it still maintains the traditions and principles of Friendly Societies, offering itself as 'Someone to watch over your money'.

Above: The ornate cover of the centenary souvenir written by Edwin Crew and published in 1926.
Left: The first Shepherds' House in Stockport.
Above left: The Order published a monthly magazine. This was the logo on the cover of the one put out in May 1940
Facing page, bottom left: The Officers and Board of Management in 1901-1902.
Facing page, right: A very attractive calendar for 1901 the original in greens and reds and much gilded. It features the Chief Shepherd, John Milne and boasts its 160,000 members. The head office in the 1900s was in Chapmen Street, Manchester

Memories of STOCKPORT

Edging out the competition

British Trimmings was founded in 1929 when Mr Alfred Stone left a family business in Kidderminster to take advantage of the flourishing hat trade in Stockport by producing trimmings for them locally.

He took premises in Compstall which his firm outgrew inside two years. He moved to Coronation Mills, Coronation Street, South Reddish. There, his business grew even in a period of recession because it diversified into trimmings for upholstery and garments. At first these were all woven but later they were knitted also.

During the Second World War the firm's machinery was adapted to make webbing and tapes for the armed forces.

In 1960 British Trimmings became a Public Limited Company but soon afterwards business declined when the stark lines of Scandinavian furniture became popular. However, that fashion passed and through the sixties and seventies the company expanded again. It bought its own dyeworks by taking over the assets of Clemesha Brothers and Birch in Leek and the firm's subsequent success attracted the attention of a much larger company Rexmore who took over British Trimmings in 1972, the same year in which British Trimmings itself bought a competitor in the industry, P. Davenport Ltd of Macclesfield. Under Rexmore the company flourished, branching out into curtain tapes, ribbons and labels.

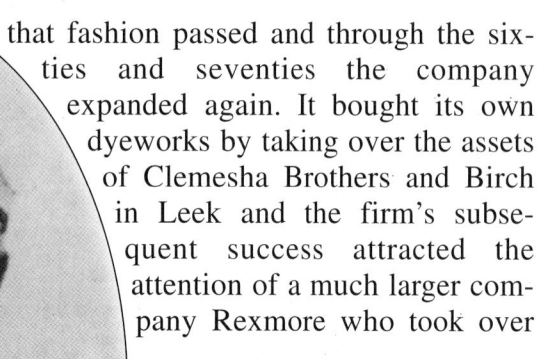

In 1983, British Trimmings was bought from Rexmore by Berisfords of Congleton who made similar products. A difficult period followed as the

Memories of STOCKPORT

Textiles of London in the following year. Both the latter firms made upholstery trimmings, girdles, lanyards and tassels.

1992 brought a need to concentrate on the core trimming business and the curtain tape department was sold to Thomas French & Sons plc. This freed capital to invest in trimming expansion.

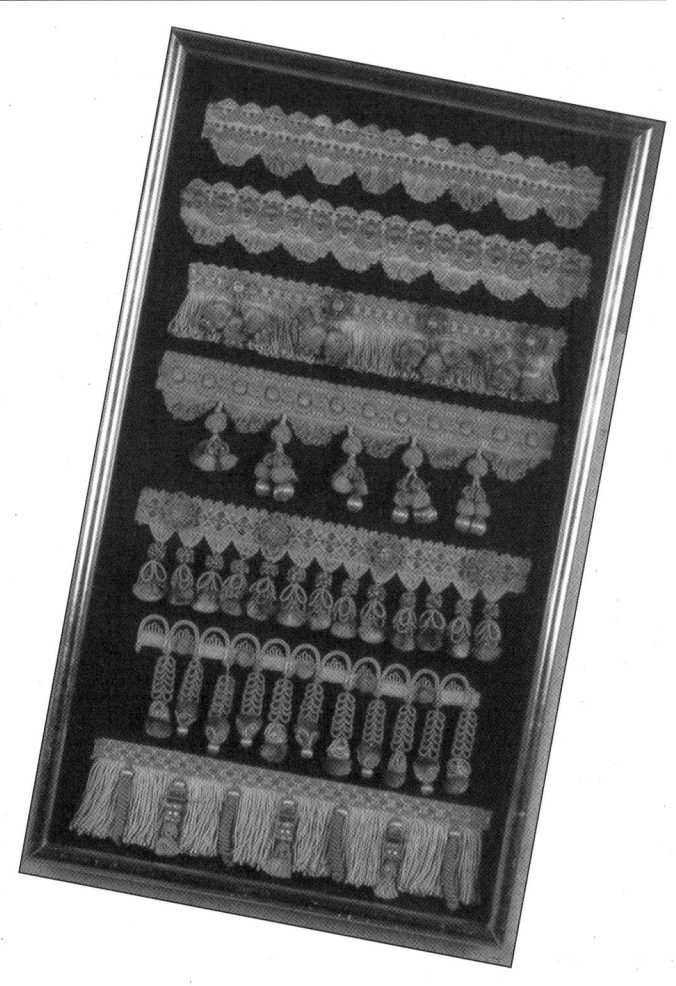

two companies rationalised. Soon afterwards Berisfords themselves were taken over by Ferguson International Holdings plc. They required the production of labels rather than trimmings so British Trimmings bought out their own business from Fergusons before buying Braidex of Peterborough in December 1988 and J Day

Facing page top Left: Alfred C. Stone who founded the company in 1929. *Facing Page Right:* The new warehouse extension in Stockport, soon after opening in 1979. *Top Left:* High-speed curtain tape looms. *Centre:* A design team discussing technical details. *Bottom:* British Trimming (Leek) Ltd, the dye house and garment trimming, manufacturing unit. *Above:* A fine display of samples of classic furnishing trimmings.

Memories of STOCKPORT

Transforming the heart of Stockport's town centre

Merseyway Shopping Centre was developed in the 1960s and spans a 400 metre length of the River Mersey as it runs through the centre of Stockport. By the late eighties the buildings within Merseyway were looking dated, no longer matching up to the high expectations of the landlord or meeting retailer demand. Customer service provision by way of car parking, public toilets and signage needed upgrading.

Hammerson UK Properties PLC, owners of Merseyway launched into a refurbishment programme which would ultimately take two years to complete, transforming the covered mall and hence maintaining Stockport as one of the most vibrant town centres in the North West. To give a good first impression, the entrances were redesigned. The old continuous canopy was done away with and a new steel and glass entrance porch was set up at the Mersey Square entrance and the vestibule was made 'double-height'. A similar entrance feature was created on Arden Walk.

The existing main mall was remodelled, with the

Above: Shoppers enjoy using the new centre.
Left: The rebuilt porch with its glazed roof over a double-height entrance. The Merseyway logo is incorporated into the glass.

Memories of STOCKPORT

existing solid roof being replaced by a glazed roof and stained glass art work. A new glass staircase led from the centre of the mall to the car parking above. The underground public toilets in the town square were scrapped and new ones built in Vernon Walk. New covered malls were created including an enclosed square at the east end of Merseyway Mall. Arden Walk was enclosed as part of this process. The Town Square entrance to the north was faced with high quality hand-made brick with stone trimming and a glazed canopy was put up to protect the shop fronts but let the light through.

Along the full length of Merseyway there was new planting and seating to make it look open and inviting. The bridge at second floor level was re-clad and the rooftop car park was redesigned to allow for extra parking.

Refurbishment was completed in May 1995. Twelve thousand additional square feet of retail space meant that units could be as big as the 1990s retailers required. The work had cost £15 million, increasing the capital value of the premises by £30 million, from £60 million to £90 million.

In the 12 months before the new complex was opened it was given maximum publicity with promotions and events for both shoppers and tenants. Red roses were handed out on St Valentine's Day and a time capsule was buried in the excavations by pupils of Reddish Vale School. Stockport people were invited to enter their old pictures of the town in a competition and they were exhibited in the Mall.

September brought a Merseyway Back to School Balloon Bonanza. A six foot mascot, Merseyway Mole stood in the middle of the mall except at Christmas when he visited hospitals in South Manchester and Stockport giving away toys and flowers.

1996 saw the commencement of the second phase of refurbishment with the emphasis on customer care.

The 900-space council-owned car park was given updated lighting and decoration, lifts were replaced and staircases upgraded. New paving has been laid in Vernon Walk and Deanery Way, whilst the stepped ramp was replaced by a new staircase that opened up the mall for shoppers.

A major new service known as 'Shopmobility'. A new lift gave access to all levels of the car park and to the shopping areas in Merseyway and the market. The scheme includes the free hire of powered scooters and wheelchairs for the disabled.

With many of Merseyway's shops and stores trading seven days a week, regular shoppers are guaranteed a service to match their every need.

Top left: *The new glazed canopy letting daylight into the shop fronts in the Town Square.*
Above: *The glazed mall has done away with the 'shut-in' feeling of older covered shopping areas.*
Left: *An interior view showing multi level facilities and the trees and shrubs that can be grown in the natural daylight.*

Memories of STOCKPORT

The Civil Defence Corps was a nationwide civilian force set up in the post war period. The onset of the cold war meant that the threat of a nuclear strike became a real concern to many governments in the west, and the main purpose of Britain's civil defence volunteers was to assist in the aftermath of such a catastrophic event. As it turned out, civil defence volunteers became involved in many incidents, working alongside the normal emergency services. One example of this was the Stockport air crash in 1967, when many passengers were led to safety by members of the Civil Defence Corps. In this picture the Mayor and mayoress of Stockport look at a civil defence exhibition in the late 1950s.

Memories of STOCKPORT

The company origins sprang from a trading house in Manchester, called Ernst Grether & company, which was formed in the late 19th century. This company dealt in various commodities and machinery throughout Europe and Mexico. Just before the First World War, the company took the name of G.W. Thornton & Co. after one of the Partners, who was Grandfather of the present Managing Director, David Thornton.

In 1926, G.W. Thornton & Son was formed by George William Thornton, and his son George, (David Thornton's father), and G.W. Thornton & Son took on part of the business of the original company, and commenced trading with Scandinavia, France, Portugal and Mexico. The company concentrated predominately on textile machinery and accessories. In 1926, G.W. Thornton & Son started importing textile machinery.

A company picnic in 1921

During the years of the Second World War, the company moved to an old, medium sized, three storey building in Cheadle which also incorporated a dairy. Initially the company rented part of the building only but subsequently the building was purchased by the Thornton Brothers. As the company expanded the dairy was bought for more accommodation and the building was expanded to its limits as the land adjoining could not be purchased.

In 1977 (incidentally the Queens Silver Jubilee year), an abandoned church and two cottages next door were purchased, demolished and the first Grether House was built on this land. G.W. Thornton & Sons Ltd remained here until 1986 when it moved to Crown Royal Industrial Park, Stockport, a small newly built trading estate where it is still situated. David Thornton joined the present Company in 1957 and was appointed as Director in 1963 and Managing Director in May 1974.

During the last fifteen years, the pattern of the textile machinery activities have changed due in part to the restructuring of the U.K. textile industry, and to changes in Principals caused by reorganisation, take-overs and expansion into new market areas.

Today the company represents a wide range of Principals covering all aspects of cloth manufacture and dyeing and finishing, with the dependency on all Principals rather than on the activities of just a small number of leading suppliers.

David Thornton: Managing Director

G. W. THORNTON & SONS LTD

Registered Office: Grether House, Crown Royal Industrial Park, Shawcross Street, Stockport, Cheshire SK1 3HB

Importers of textile and other machinery

TEXTILE MACHINERY WORLDWIDE FOR OVER A HUNDRED YEARS

Tel: 0161 477 1010 Fax: 0161 477 9144

Memories of STOCKPORT

A FAMILY RUN BUSINESS, OFFERING A TRADITIONAL, FRIENDLY AND PERSONAL SERVICE THAT HAS BEEN SECOND TO NONE FOR OVER THIRTY YEARS

This family furnishing firm was started in the late 1940's by Mr George Bryant using premises at 818 Stockport Road in Levenshulme. By the late 1960's the firm was outgrowing its local warehouse and eventually bought the ex-Wright & Green warehouse on Manchester Road in Heaton Norris. This was modernised

═Bryants of Stockport═

BRYANT HOUSE, WELLINGTON ROAD NORTH, STOCKPORT

Secure Storage * Expert Service *
Competitive Prices * Self Packing *
Airport Car Storage * Furniture Retail

Removals & Storage
Furniture & Carpet Retail

TELEPHONE 0161 477 4321 OR FAX 0161 476 6232

Above: This picture of Station Road, Cheadle Hulme probably dates from the 1930s with the road only half of its present width. The Elysium cinema has the extended entrance in the centre; this is now our Shopping Arcade. (Berger's on the right corner is still there, albeit now as a dry cleaning firm).

and extended and served until the late 1980's, coping with eight retail outlets. The large ex-National Carriers (and before that railway goods) warehouse on the A6 was then acquired, along with the ex-Vic Moores shop as a retail outlet. (These premises had originally housed the Autovac car fuel pump manufactory). The warehouse provides an ideal base for the storage and removal business which it now contains. In the meantime, the retail side was superbly accommodated in the converted Elysium cinema on Station Road, Cheadle Hulme, which is well worth a visit, being a shopping arcade on three floors with a cafeteria. The extensive furniture and carpet showrooms offer a very wide choice of high quality stock or goods to order, and our knowledgeable and courteous staff will be pleased to serve you.

Memories of STOCKPORT

Gresty's FLOWER SERVICES

Gresty's had their first encounter with business about 75 years ago when Ernest Gresty, the present owner's grandfather, grew flowers and other produce in Northenden, Manchester. It was truly a family affair as various members of the family were involved in one way or another at the time.

Ernest's son, also called Ernest and his wife, Marjorie sold their wares at the Stockport Markets in the 1940s and in the early 1950s, when they won first prize in a Civic Week competition (see picture below). Around this time, they opened the shop at Castle Street, Edgeley which is still in use today.

Ernest had four children, a son, (Ernie) and three daughters (Pauline, Susan and Hazel). Ernie and Pauline began working in the shop from school, followed soon after by the other two sisters. This close association has never altered. The family still work side-by-side with each other, along with other family members, including Pauline's daughter, Lorrie. Today, besides the family, about twenty other people work at Gresty's.

Business was soaring and it soon became clear that new premises were needed. The branch at Wellington Road South was opened in early 1994. Coincidentally, soon afterwards the Castle Street shop was gutted by fire started by arsonists. This branch re-opened, refurbished and better than ever. Following the success of the Wellington Road South branch they reluctantly decided to close their market stall, which had been trading for over 50 years. This gave the owners a chance to concentrate on developing the two shops for the future.

Above: This photograph shows Marjorie Gresty surrounded by Pauline, Ernie, Susan and Hazel and 1000 red roses. It was taken before a charity ballet evening, one of the many interesting and challenging events they have been involved with since the business was started. *Left:* The presentation of First Prize to the Gresty family during Civic Week in 1952.

262 Wellington Road South, Heaviley, Stockport.
8 - 10 Castle Street, Edgeley, Stockport.
TEL: 0161 480 0500 / 0161 480 0112

true north
HOLDINGS

If you have enjoyed this book, why not try the others in the popular "Memories" series?

Memories of Bolton

Memories of Blackburn

Memories of Oldham

Memories of Preston

Memories of Rochdale

You can order any of these books through good local book shops, price £4.99. Alternatively we can mail a book to any UK address for £6.00 including first class postage. To arrange a postal copy please 'phone 01422 344344 or write to us at True North, 117 Dean Clough, Halifax, HX3 5AX.

CO-OPERATIVE FUNERAL SERVICES

Pay for your funeral now and your family won't pay for it later.

When people don't plan ahead for their own funerals it is their loved ones who have to make the decisions and meet the financial burden. That's why it is sensible and practical to plan for your funeral now.

With a Co-operative Funeral Bond you can tailor-make funeral arrangements at today's prices. No further costs will be incurred regardless of when the funeral takes place. There are no hidden extras. So when your loved one needs us, we'll be there to carry out your wishes and they won't have to meet the cost.

F·O·S
FUNERAL ONBUDSMAN SCHEME

fsc

INVESTORS IN PEOPLE

Manchester Road, Heaton Chapel, Stockport SK4 5DH
Telephone: 0161-432 0818
95 Manchester Road, Denton, Manchester M34 2AF
Telephone: 0161-320 7812